Terracom Poet Series

I0162776

Rime

William Driscoll

Terracom Books

Rime
Terracom Books Poetry Series/March 2014
First Edition

Published by Terracom Books
A Division of Terracom Media

ISBN−13: 978−0−615−96864−3

Terracom Media

mediaterracom@gmail.com
Snow

CONTENTS

The Academy – The Salon (and Mr. Manet)

The Academy

To be a master's
a mighty road
of the finer arts
to teach the way
to express oneself
in the accepted mode
ever precise
with just a touch
of gray

To see the eager
student faces
look to me
to guide their art
to all the welcome
familiar places
(though they may
never set
the puzzle to
half so well
as me or you)

And it is comfy
here, I say
the salary, awards

the public viewing

with all my peers

to share my way

don't ask me

why

the–average–guy's

pooh–poohing

The Salon

We show the art

that's fit to see

within our bounds

eternally free

We know the art

that's fit, you see

within our bounds

naturally

And if you push

the bounds, like we

we're ever on

the edge, you see

we'll welcome you

with corps d'esprit

Within our bounds

naturally

We show the art
that's fit to see
come see the art
come see, come see

We know the art
that's fit, mais oui
within our bounds
naturally

And if you like
our edge, like we
we're ever on
the edge, you see
we'll welcome you
enthusiastically

Within our bounds
naturally

Mr. Manet snarled:

No!

Mr. Manet sang:

O! to take my
heart in hand
brush colors flat
and bold and hasty

to take my subjects

from life again

without the permission

of the Academy

without the nod

of the Salon

to brush the candid

colors on!

Mr. Manet laughed:

Venez au Salon des

Refusés! mes amis...[1]

---

1 - Come to the show of the refused! my friends...

An Eggstremelybad Mentalcase

(or extreme unguent)

Some kitschy old alias hack

came on with a thwackety thwack

but to my bemuse

the thuddle extru–

ded juice from his backety back

de dum dum!

non quis, sed quid[2]

Mr. Cott drank a lot

shot by shot

he'd thank a lot

slur by slur

it became a blur

as fart by fart

he stank a lot

Mr. Cott once paint a lot

pinks and greens

he'd feint a lot

cherub faces

and boobs a lot

curving hips

and thews a lot

Mr. Cott regret a lot

that life was

so coquette a lot

and beauty brought

on debt a lot

so Mr. Cott would

fret a lot

---

2 - not who, but what

Mr. Dobson drank a lot
and cavorted with the
Frank a lot
he loved the waiter's
wife a lot
he loved her all his
life a lot

Mr. D. was taught a lot
that life was filled with
fraught a lot
and work's the way to
win a lot
to help avoid the
sin a lot

But Mr. D. he shirked his lot
and scribbled verse or
worse a lot
he liked to watch the
stars a lot
to visit seedy
bars a lot

Mr. D. bemoaned his lot
that he was left
alone a lot

to sing sad songs of

wrongs a lot

he tied the hangman's

knot a lot

Noblins

The Noblins practice
the art of knifery
knavishly noodlin'
their raw—flamin's slicery
slavishly poodlin'
their saw—gnawin's micery
the Noblins practice
the art of knifery

These gasbags scale
the heights of hackery
thwacking their critics
with donnish thwackery
nebulous misty and
fogging perfwackery
these gasbags scale
the heights of hackery

These putty—mouths potter
with painless prufanity
constantly uttering
aneless inanities
Blake as a blister
and rhyme as insanity
these putty—mouths potter
with painless prufanity

These Noblins are brawlin'
with hopes that are fallin'
or ogres that cost 'em
a tall belly crawlin'
or hasty—held hatreds
too small to be sprawlin'
these Noblins are brawlin'
with hopes that are fallin'

These minnows feel mighty
in teeny glass bowls
or cellophaned dixie cups
dotted with holes
with lãssez fãire morals
the right fit for trolls
true minnows feel mighty
in teeny glass bowls

And we watchers?
we dodgers?
watch—on with élan
and study these Noblins
like bugs on a pond
when all we would wish
is for them to respond
and promise they'll muddy
our ponds with aplomb

Filadalay

Filadalay went lumping down

he lumped to town

he lumped to town

there to sell

his apples sweet

but on the way a few did eat

he ate a few

and then some more

until he'd gobbled up a score

then Filadalay

sat glumping down

he never made it into town

Filadalay got up to say

this has been

the best of days

and for these apples

I give praise

then he went lumping

on his way

he lumped his way

he lumped his way

did our blessed Filadalay

Mon Captain Naught

Mon Captain Naught
was a tyrannical gent
so clever and crafty
the words he spent
sharp as a tack
and profane as a draught
and in love with himself
was Mon Captain Naught

His black ship, smallish
was filled with holes
his whip–sails
webs on spindle poles
bestride his nest
he swaggered and taught
and chastened his critics
Mon Captain Naught

From 'hind his (bull)work
he'd hide, and blame
the stupidity of others
for smudging his fame
he'd shrivel his enemies:
the good, the nice
and rule his wee world
a giant among mice

Mon Captain Naught

would throw a fit

if anyone dared

to question his wit

for behind his bristle

a soft–heart fraught

our very so sensitive

Mon Captain Naught

A Bust of Wilde

For the slap and tickle poemlet

you brooked no erstwhile peer

with now no gaol to hold it

no Housman pity here

Koniology

You may not see them
dancing there
but they are dancing
in the air
niggling, prickling
nagging you
between the sitcom
and the shew
between the innings
and the song
floating there
they dance along

You're fat, you're lazy
stupid, drugs
between the talk shows
and the plugs
wear condoms, seat belts
stop the hate
you've too much taters
on your plate
you've too much butter
on your corn
they're floating there
from night to morn

You may not hear them

nagging there

but they are nagging

everywhere

don't smoke you fatso

reprobate

do I see french fries

on your plate?

you want to drink

that drano true?

so here's a label

just for you

Admit you left

that doggy–doo

beside your neighbor's

portmanteau

are you a nit–wit

with no nit?

we'll fine you

for that doggy sh__!

Yes, they are dancing

everywhere

dancing, dancing

in the air

at all us fatso

imbeciles
so safe within
our domiciles

I Wanna be a Feminist Man

I argue against my own kind

docker shorts, a taut behind

touchy feely déclassé

all the chicks dig me that way

All Boxed In

I put a box around my life
to keep it straight and neat
at six a.m. I exercise
then have some toast to eat
then off to work
then eat again
then work, then eat again
and then it's on to TV
and nodding in the den
I get eight hours sleep
you see
then do it all again

My greatest fears, you wonder?
are doubting my answers many
or spending a nickel
perish the thought!
when I could have spent
a penny
or not being thin
or eating some fat
I've no use for that, not I
or smoking or drinking liquor
or eating chocolate pie

My box is prim and comfy
it keeps things set and tidy

on Sundays I go off to church

at night I wear a nightie

I mow the lawn

or rake the leaves

or shovel snow on Saturday

I flush with joy

to paint the house

I blush at any flattery

I fill my hours with work

you see

and never have a sadder—day

Will I ever leave this box?

I will

there's another that's waiting

for me

and a plot that's dark

and vacant

beneath a shady tree

yes! when this last lid closes

that silently waits for me

I'll finally have

what I've cherished the most

some true security

The Naffoo Bird Sings

In a tree in the baynans
the Naffoo Bird sings
too–lay, too–lay, too–lay

From sundown to sun–up
he throws back his wings
too–lay, too–lay, too–lay

In the sapphire twilight
as echoes appear
too–lay, too–lay, too–lay

The Naffoo bird preens
as his lover is near
too–lay, too–lay, too–lay

O what can one think?
(the poor Naffoo is wrong)
too–lay, too–lay, too–lay

Of this silly little bird
in love with his song
too–lay, too–lay, too–lay

A Plea to the Passionless

The brain's the organ
of romance
not either gender
in your pants
though when they meet
momentary face
the world's a less
unpleasant place

Without the weight
of wisdom's will
the forbidden comes
a sugar pill
to young lovers who
will never know
the surging joy of
passion's flow

The joy of those
content to wait
to suffer through
that longing ache
then join like eagles
in their throw
they will know
raw passion's flow

So, hook–up at binge bars

if you must

but never feel

the rising lust

of lover's who will

ride the course

of passion's surging

bulging horse

We judge not cynics

by their spleen

nor puffy–bullies

by their boil

why judge romantics

by their toil?

why judge romantics

by their toil?

The Rag–a–man

Raggedy raggedy rag–a–man
can see the way the ladies can
can raise an oy! with the hoi poloi
can walk in duo–diapan

Raggedy raggedy rag–a–man
can see beyond that old trash can
to where the river holds the sea
and currents out to old Taipan

Raggedy raggedy rag–a–man
will whisper with the stars and land
tells secrets in the mermaid's ear
and yanks the holohedral band

Raggedy raggedy rag–a–man
will tip the bottle in his hand
and tell you life's a jolly game
then thumb his nose at the mori–band

Dem Beans

Dem beans

dem beans

dem

navy beans

Dem beans

dem beans

dem

kidney beans

Dem beans

dem beans

dem

pinto beans

Dem beans

dem beans

dem beans

I've tried on Shirts

I've tried on shirts
I've tried on pants
been fairy–married
and learned to dance
I've tried to grasp
this thing and that
to zip my fly
and tip my hat
but all that noise
I've hailed as so
and all those truths
I've rushed to know
have brought me here
to this far place near
where worries
are scurried
with pretzels and beer
and naked I stand
with this truth
in my hand
that this land is me
and I am the land
and chance I glance
in a blue–pool sea
that child again!
why, yes! – that's me!

The Walrus and the Debutante

'The time has come'

the Walrus thought

'to go shopping for

a debutante

a little laughing

waspish thing

to turn my summer

into spring

my taste's a garden

overgrown

I'll have one for my

very own'

So to the market

waddled he

he rubbed his chubby

fists with glee

'I'll need a sprig

of basil too

and cormeran

and tarraru

and pink young taters

for my stew'

he chortled in the

morning dew

The bump and smell

of Walrus town

that buzzing murmur

all around

him as he made

his way with care

to the walrus'

market square

brought back to him

the rainy days

the never ending

wainy ways

that make a belly

an empty ache

as he waddled 'round

that marketplace

Where in the open

market's air

hung debutantes

there by their hair

some soft and fuzzy

like a pear

while others straight

and liny—air

while all around

the bobbing wares

the walrus men

went by in pairs

ogg–l–ing

some dainty dish

like seal meat

or silver fish

'For years I've saved

my se–al pelts

a life's worth

towards this

day of wealth

and now I'll have

my hunger sate

upon a shinning

golden plate!'

sneered our walrus

as he stroked

a massive tusk

and then he poked

a roundish waif

and likewise pinched

a curving ado–

lescent inch

'I'll take this here'

the walrus sneered

and his fellow walri

gathered 'round

then with some shears

a sack appeared
and soon his prize
was neatly bound
he paid his skins out
lovingly
those pelts he'd saved
so frugally
then o'er his shoulder
the struggling–sack
he craned
and went back to his
house again

He set his table
with a flair
his finest china
his silverware
he cut his taters
just a few
and lovingly
prepared his stew
and when his prize
was skinned and boned
he sat down to his
feast alone
to days of feasting
rushing by
on soft deb–breast
on kidney pie

On juicy thighs

or shoulder roast

or lady fingers

boned on toast

he greedily

engorged his prize

but for her

remarkable eyes

so clear and young

as if near

to speak a word

or shed a tear

sanguine and pure

the color of wheat

he laid them on

the board to eat

he laid them on

the board to eat

but kept them there

for so they seemed

small pearls to haunt

a walri's dreams

The days went by

like a jester's grin

but instead of fat

our 'rus grew thin

and thinner as he

ate and ate

and greedily

relieved his plate

for his hunger grew

it grew so pure

(that gruff and gruesome

epicure)

his skin hung loose

all folded 'round

it practically

assailed the ground

So, to the market

shuffled he

who had no hope

nor remedy

and ghost–like languored

in that square

two eyes, one hunger

one despair

a soul of dire

impoverishment

a form of rife

diminishment

a heart of longing

mind of pain

he stumbled to his

house again

And there he found

those two small eyes

the remnants of

his priceless prize

starring at him

as if to note

these words of wisdom

and I quote

"Some remedies are

worse than...disease"

old Publilius Syrus

was known to gloat –

the walrus then

fell on his knees

and with a sigh

he did emote

that 'all in all

my hunger's spent!'

cried the walrus to the

debutante

Safe Sonnetry

(a poetic health warning)

Alert as morning's hue arises a daring
Bud, bedogged with dew–drops of desire's
O'er–arching attention straightening skyward rearing
Eyeward, that little soldier's crown perspires

A liquor deadlier than the cobra's spleen
Till that valiant disk doth intercede a'twixt, that gold
–en disk unrolled! o'er thy passion's purple glean
Of ghastly abab's and cdcd's a' mixed

But is best best if no more interwove?
Is the squealer from the country lance assured?
Where the warming tongue, those golden globes of love?
Once welcome–arched, now long ago demurred

From this thy self–infected ghostly lover
May my latex–chiding help your rash(i)ness recover

I Never Conjured your Eyes

I never conjured your eyes

when I could see them

should I cast them orbs

or loam or whey?

I never invoked your lips

when I could blend them

into mine: cherries? honey?

who's to say

I never climbed the mountains

of your breasts in verse

where the moonlight lights

the valley white beneath

such crowns of idol–bronze

where spirits rise

to summon tremors

in my thighs

were I to give you

the immortality

your beauties earn

would you get lost!

and let my peace return?

Sen Zala Ben

Sen zala ben went the melatanel

Sen zala ben za lay

All through the Kala the nelenboleven

Went click crackle clutter

And tick tackle crackle

And sputtered and hackled all day

Lon all the great Gala the toysomeness

Grinkle and tempastious Tala did join

Di gorfed the gree gumbets

And slurfed ninalivin

Sen zala ben zala za lay

Don Kor the gray grinkle

Di tapped his orn torbin

And grudrily worbled a cee

Of lindinleer lirmon

Zorn and druge termon

Sen zala ben zala za lay

Injy to sorey twor the melatanel

As the safir turned into the dwim

The Grinkle and Tala

All through the great Kala

Eyes wory and shluzing all immy and zuzing

Went trussling and woozing to sprig

Di deemed the gree deems of mov ninalivin

Sneegling through the soray

Tillin den goring when the nelenboleven

Would click crackle clutter

And tick tackle crackle

And sputter and hackle all day

Rime

Rime rime jangle and jime
time line pine a dime
hind rind scratch a lime
rime rime jangle and jime

Rime zest a–lotta pest
rest jest abandoned nest
pressed crest cats undressed
rime zest a–lotta pest

Rime snooze lathe and lose
blues ruse concrete shoes
thews cruise bashed and bruised
rime snooze lathe and lose

Rime rime jingle and jame
tame lame pinch a mame
hame reign niggle and blame
rime rime jingle and jame

Mulligan

Mulligan
began again
plowing up the
land again
chewing up
a stand of trees
with his known
ferocity

Stumps and branches
clotting there
like bleeding scalp
and matted hair
a rended scar of
earth and mud
of bloody muck and
pine–sap blood

There all the woods
that once held sway
he carted to
the mill for pay
to press into
a host of things

from toilet rolls

to shower rings

From little gnomes

with painted eyes

to bright red boxes

for French Fries

to tiki lamps

for backyard fun

he ground it down

for everyone

When Mulligan

had done his thing

the owners plowed

the earth again

piling up the

shattered bones

the broken boughs

the brown pinecones

And in the barren

scar they dropped

a pile er two

of broken rocks

a beat up car

on cinder blocks

a chest er two

with rusty locks

Tweedle-dum and Tweedle-dee

Tweedle–dum and tweedle–dee
lived together secretly
loved a love they
dare not name
night by night
they loved again

Tweedle–dum and tweedle–dee
loved with sinful ecstasy
iniquity upon iniquity
they gathered to
themselves with glee

Then one day
the Tweedles heard
with utter shock
they got the word
that their sin
was just a way –
like the other's
sloppy play

Utterly dejected then
they went their separate
ways again
what fun is there
in normalcy?

in bourgeoisies'
complacency?

Tweedle–dum and tweedle–dee
ennuied their own
monotonies
for life, in truth's
so very hard
when you're no longer
avant–garde!

Househusband

Weed the garden

clean the pool

get the children

off to school

Beat the rugs

clean the van

fry the bacon

in the pan

(and still have

enough

to make her feel

like a man!)

A woman may work

from sun to sun

but a househusband's

work is never done

Rhodes' Colossus

Rhodes' Colossus
into shields is made
the Pharos gone
to build a mosque
golden Zeus
has been bought and spent
for entertainment
and for rent
the Sphinx's nose
an emperor's toil
Athena's centaurs
colonial spoil
Artemis' virgin's chambers
must
be uncovered from
time's covered dust

But down the years
some powerful rhyme
has stood the decaying
test of time
and as Homer's Helen
that beauty prove
who was the object
of their love

Were I to add you to

this firmament

would you mind so much

to pay my rent?

though money and I

we seldom speak

my love for you's as strong

as any Greek

When y'touch Things

When y'touch things
but not things you
can love the seen
and unseen too
when people around y'
are vital and new
then come back
to me me darlin'

When laughter's the norm
and not your goal
and sweet truth has tilt
your axis pole
when y'are gathered
concrete and whole
then return
to me me darlin'

As scaly old snakes
their rough skins shed
and butterflies break
from a caterpillar's head
when y'can see
what y'll be when you're dead
I'll wait
for ye me darlin'

Now as I made ye

bright and stout

condemned to wear

your concepts out

until y'see

without a doubt

that ye

are me me darlin

A Nigerian Story

(of Edshu, their trickster/creator god)

A brother and sister

in their fields

one day

each on their side

of that dusty road

saw Edshu

walking on his way

tall as grain

the hat upon his head

on one side blue

the other red

then having passed

the god returned

turning there

his hat around

laughing as he

went to town

'Did you see that god

my brother my

his hat as blue as

a summer sky?'

'Nonsense, sister

your eyes are crossed

his hat was red as

summers lost.'

Was blue

was red

and back

and to

that hat

on head

was red

was blue

Then brother

thumped the other

thump!

And sister

bumped the other

bump!

Thump bump!

poke bite!

tap slap!

full fight!

hair pull!

nip twist!on jaw!

full fist!

They fought

till blood–dust

covered their
head
'cause one
saw blue
the other
red

Well, late
that night
before the King
(who'd never heard
of such a thing)
there just before
their sentencing
Edshu appeared
hat in sight
and said that he'd
explain their fight

'Know this then
forgive me do
I really meant
no harm to you
spreading strife
is what I do –
fact your peace lost
is my joy's profiting'
and laughing this
he poked the King

'Humph' humphed

the King

as burbles raced

all about

their judgment place

still Edshu was heard

to chuckle as he

left their sullen

company

'Curse me then

if you wish

you see

I gave you

the ability'